What animal is it?

Written by Becca Heddle

Collins

Look at the snapshots for hints.
Turn to check you were correct.

This animal has damp skin with black spots.

It's a poison dart frog. It inhabits forests in Brazil.

This animal swims and blends in with rocks.

It's a squid. It can pump out ink.

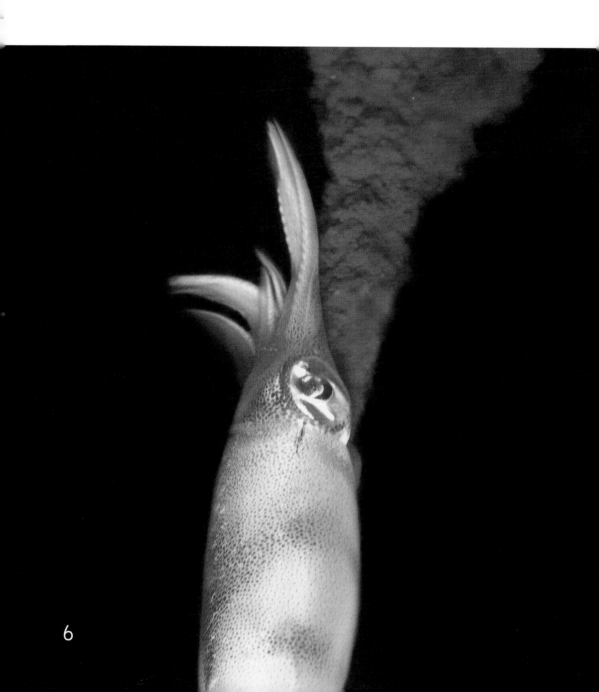

This animal is black and hunts at dusk.

It's a bat. It flaps in forests.

This animal is strong with black fur.

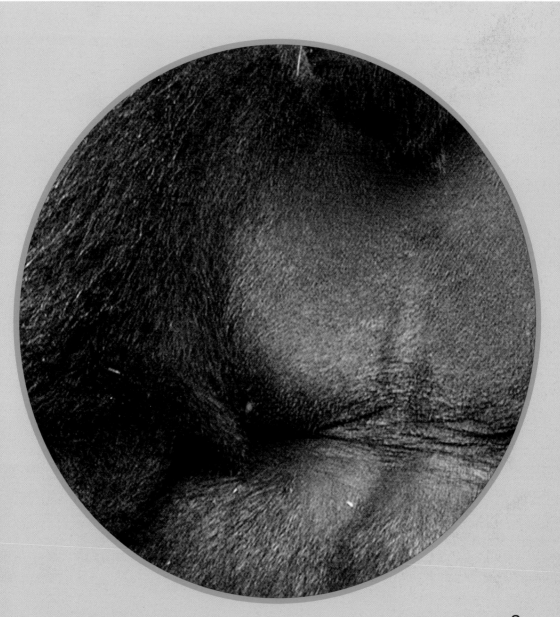

It's a gorilla. It inhabits forests in Africa.

This animal lifts its crest to express itself.

It's an umbrella cockatoo.
It inhabits rainforests.

Were you correct? Did you spot the animals?

Animals

After reading

Letters and Sounds: Phase 4

Word count: 100

Focus on adjacent consonants with short vowel phonemes, e.g. /c/r/e/s/t

Common exception words: the, to, you, were, out, what

Curriculum links (EYFS): Understanding the World

Curriculum links (National Curriculum, Year 1): Science: Animals, including humans

Early learning goals: Reading: read and understand simple sentences, use phonic knowledge to decode regular words and read them aloud accurately

National Curriculum learning objectives: Spoken language: listen and respond appropriately to adults and their peers; Reading/word reading: read other words of more than one syllable that contain taught GPCs; Reading/comprehension: understand both the books they can already read accurately and fluently and those they listen to by checking that the text makes sense to them as they read, and correcting inaccurate reading

Developing fluency

- Your child may enjoy hearing you read the book.
- Model reading a spread with lots of expression so that it sounds interesting to the listener. Now ask your child to choose a spread and do the same thing.

Phonic practice

- Practise reading words with more than one syllable together. Ask your child to read the following word: **inhabits**.
- Ask your child how many syllables the word has. They could clap for each syllable.
- Now do the same with the following words: correct, animal, snapshots.

Extending vocabulary

- Read your child each of the following sets of words. Can your child find the odd one out in each set?

  inhabits   lives   animal   (*animal*)

  right   sleeps   correct   (*sleeps*)

  strong   hunts   searches (*strong*)